VOICE

The little book of an Executive Coach's Wisdom

Dean Williams

Grosvenor House
Publishing Limited

All rights reserved
Copyright © Dean Williams, 2017

The right of Dean Williams to be identified as the author of this
work has been asserted in accordance with Section 78
of the Copyright, Designs and Patents Act 1988

The book cover picture is copyright to Dean Williams

This book is published by
Grosvenor House Publishing Ltd
Link House
140 The Broadway, Tolworth, Surrey, KT6 7HT.
www.grosvenorhousepublishing.co.uk

This book is sold subject to the conditions that it shall not,
by way of trade or otherwise, be lent, resold, hired out or
otherwise circulated without the author's or publisher's prior
consent in any form of binding or cover other than that in
which it is published and without a similar condition including
this condition being imposed
on the subsequent purchaser.

A CIP record for this book
is available from the British Library

ISBN 978-1-78623-897-9

"A Coach is part adviser, part sounding board, part cheer-leader, part manager and part strategist." – *The Business Journal*

ABOUT THE AUTHOR

Acclaimed in the UK's *Sunday Times* newspaper for global business coaching, and a member of the prestigious Forbes Coaches Council, Dean is a regular columnist for a wide-variety of business publications and author of two previous books: *Thrive: How To Achieve And Sustain High-level Career Success;* and *Creating Grade A Business Relationships.* Dean is also a co-founder of The Business Coaching Academy, which he set up to educate and enlighten managers and leaders on the art of coaching.

The majority of Dean's time is allocated to working with executives and boards, offering them one-to-one and team coaching, as well as career counselling and mentoring. In the last 17 years he has amassed 3,000 coaching sessions with top-level executives. Dean boasts a client list that includes several blue-chip corporations – Samsung, HSBC, Barclays, MasterCard and BUPA to name but a few.

ACKNOWLEDGEMENTS

With huge thanks to...

The wonderful Mrs W. for the third time!

To Richard and Ian for helping to inspire and for offering strength and direction 17 years ago.

THE ESSENCE OF VOICE

Essentially this book is a replay of 100 actual coaching sessions that were conducted through a calendar year.

The book provides a record and reflection of significant and memorable interventions during each session; be it questions (from a 'pure coaching' approach), challenge or implants of wisdom – an Executive Coach's voice!

It is effectively a Coach's diary. Brevity is applied, for each of the sessions a brief scenario and context is given – followed by the Coach's 'voice'. The latter not being a full manuscript of the conversation, more the moment that made the difference; those light bulb moments!

Confidentiality is of course intact. Coaching notes are not over sanitised to stay true to the sessions.

This book will prove insightful to both existing and developing coaches, but also to any leader or manager that wants to develop their conversational style and impact!

Enjoy!

#1

CONTEXT OF SESSION

Readying a Head Of Marketing for an Interim Director role – discussing the need to persuade senior stakeholders to appoint from within rather than look externally ...

> COACH'S VOICE
>
> Let them know you want it. Promote the benefits you can bring in your candidacy, as well as how you would mitigate the risks they currently see in the position being vacated. What is your competitive advantage versus an external candidate? Be specific; be ready to outline your 30-, 60-, 90-day plan. Comfort will aid their decision.

#2

CONTEXT OF SESSION

Helping someone tackle their anxiety for preparing to deliver a presentation ...

> **COACH'S VOICE**
>
> Focus on the first 60 seconds of the presentation. Nail it. Start well and the momentum carries you. If a footballer starts a game with a series of nice touches - they are likely to have a great game.
>
> Less is often more. Focus on the rule of three - three areas/points to deliver. Use your physicality to demonstrate and engage the audience. For example; use your fingers to demonstrate progress against the three areas/points.

#3

CONTEXT OF SESSION

In helping somebody tackle an individual's unproductive behaviour ...

> COACH'S VOICE
>
> Don't focus on the behaviour alone, focus and understand the intention that led to that behaviour - seek to understand. Only then can you truly help.

#4

CONTEXT OF SESSION

In helping somebody accept feedback that they should manage their impatience for listening to others without interrupting ...

> COACH'S VOICE
>
> Understand that everyone likes to finish. Don't let your passion and drive become an overplayed strength. Practice 'pattern interrupts' (intelligent questioning) to bring the conversation back on point if necessary.

#5

CONTEXT OF SESSION

In helping an ambitious lady build her resilience in the face of perceived jealousy from peers ...

> **COACH'S VOICE**
>
> Often others can feel exposed by those that show high levels of ambition. That's their problem not yours. It's not a reason to lose ambition - it's a reality check and something to accept. Get comfortable with the discomfort. Do understand that ambition isn't for everyone!

#6

CONTEXT OF SESSION

Counselling a Director having difficulty analysing whether to accept a lucrative job offer or stay with his current organisation ...

> COACH'S VOICE
>
> The other company will court you – why would they not? Expect to be blown away with the offer. But what is it that would keep you here? What are you not prepared to lose?

#7

CONTEXT OF SESSION

In helping a Vice-President consider the impact of his 'strained and emotional' relationship with another individual ...

> COACH'S VOICE
>
> People won't always remember everything you say, but they will always remember how you make them feel!
>
> Articulation with over emotion doesn't work; the message will be lost and your emotion is the only thing people will see!

#8

CONTEXT OF SESSION

In helping an individual come out of a strained relationship with their departing line manager, reporting to another ...

> COACH'S VOICE
>
> You've got used to playing 'politics' (navigating around your line manager). Ensure this is not the learnt behavioural pattern with your new boss - start fresh, expect alignment and synergies.

#9

CONTEXT OF SESSION

In helping a Director 'process' a tricky exit from an organisation ...

> COACH'S VOICE
>
> Be aware of the importance of a clean exit! Distance yourself from unproductive conversations, control your triggers, and let your clean exit enable positive momentum into your new organisation. Don't carry disappointment in how you reacted in your final days into your new role.

#10

CONTEXT OF SESSION

In helping a Director who has controlling attributes to delegate more ...

> COACH'S VOICE
>
> Think about your motivation to change your habits! What does delegating more effectively enable you to do for the business? Your team? Yourself? The right motivation leads to sustainable habit!

#11

CONTEXT OF SESSION

In helping a Head Of adjust to the news of a large restructure ...

> COACH'S VOICE
>
> **Head Of**: "I'm resigned to whatever happens to me happens to me" ...
>
> **Coach**: "Let me play that back. What does that sound like?"
>
> **Head Of**: "The words of a victim!"
>
> **Coach**: "What's the impact of that?"
>
> **Head Of**: "Not great!"
>
> **Coach**: "Let's find some tangible actions that put you back in the game. Let's lessen those voices in your head!"

#12

CONTEXT OF SESSION

In helping an individual adjust to some rather challenging 360º feedback from direct reports ...

> COACH'S VOICE
>
> Let's walk through the report. Tell me what developmental feedback you recognise as fair and true? What are you prepared to action?

#13

CONTEXT OF SESSION

Witnessing and helping an individual take the learning from a tough first meeting as a Chair ...

> COACH'S VOICE
>
> Think pull rather than push. How can you get them to want to climb the mountain? Get them on-side earlier - ask questions to determine expectations, thought process and motivations.

#14

CONTEXT OF SESSION

In helping a member of a senior leadership team position their frustrations about their role in a positive frame to their Managing Director ...

> COACH'S VOICE
>
> Think about where the frustrations are coming from. If you are frustrated because of your motivation for the role - that's positive, isn't it? Use this to pre-frame the conversation with the MD. Come armed with solutions/options.

#15

CONTEXT OF SESSION

In helping a newly crowned leader to effectively deal with consistent apathy from two of their direct reports ...

> COACH'S VOICE
>
> Don't compromise on standards and behaviours, don't sacrifice your role to do theirs! It's important that you start off tight and then learn to loosen up in your management style – once you see the right behaviours!

#16

CONTEXT OF SESSION

In counselling a Director to continue to build connections with his fractious team after a bitter 12 months ...

> ### COACH'S VOICE
>
> Focus on the future. The past is the past. Develop an objective as a team – to be the best you can be. Open a communication line with the whole team encouraging 'feed forward' – if we want to be the best we can be ... what do we as a team need to do differently, do more of, do less of? As the leader recognise the part you play in the success or failure and elicit feedback from the team. As the leader you go first.

#17

CONTEXT OF SESSION

In helping a Head Of being promoted to a Director, develop a strategy for uplifting their base remuneration on the back of a 'disappointing' offer letter received ...

> COACH'S VOICE
>
> Where was your expectation? Sell it to me! Think about three boxes (boxes A, B and C) - box A represents 'what you'd be ecstatic to get', box B 'what you would be happy to get', and box C 'what you would accept as a minimum'. Playing with box A only - sell your story and rationale in line with your request. Sell your rationale before talking figures! Keep the other boxes hidden!

#18

CONTEXT OF SESSION

Speaking with an individual going for an internal senior promotion, reluctant to 'profile build' in an explicit way ...

> COACH'S VOICE
>
> Think about how we can get senior stakeholders to see more of your quality and leadership style without you shouting from the rooftops! For example, championing a project of true value to your business. A high value project will provide you with a platform to demonstrate your ability in a pragmatic way. Remember your external competitors for the role are likely to sell their profile! Take nothing for granted!

#19

CONTEXT OF SESSION

In helping a manager push back on his team coming to him with challenges ...

> **COACH'S VOICE**
>
> Beware the 'monkeys' on your back! Stop being the 'consultant' – fixing their problems for them. Wear a different hat from time to time – wear the coaching hat. Question, challenge and encourage them to think through their own dilemma. The answer to most challenges lies within the individual.

#20

CONTEXT OF SESSION

In helping a newly appointed senior leader transition from doing to leading after an initial struggle ...

> COACH'S VOICE
>
> In a sentence, explain what your role is now and how it differs from what you were doing in your previous role. How much of that are you doing right now? What should you be doing differently? What should you let go of?

#21

CONTEXT OF SESSION

In helping an ambitious Head Of position himself for a Director role ...

> COACH'S VOICE
>
> Who will be important in the selection process? (The Board). What is the Board's perception of you right now? (Unknown). We need them to see the same quality you bring into our interactions. How could you increase your visibility with them? Exposure carries risk and reward – the interview process starts now!

#22

CONTEXT OF SESSION

In helping a newly appointed Director Of Marketing transition into a new company operating within an unaccustomed culture ...

> COACH'S VOICE
>
> Don't lose you in the transition! Bring your strengths and your difference. Different doesn't mean wrong! Mimicking only what you see from others is not sustainable. Back your track record and approach.

#23

CONTEXT OF SESSION

Advising a Finance Director on how to process and adjust to an 'interfering' and 'intimidating' senior stakeholder ...

> COACH'S VOICE
>
> One option you have is to re-frame how you think and feel about the 'interference'. Rather than see it as a negative motivator 'I must not get this wrong or' ... consider balancing with 'his interference is making me sharp and on point – helping me to be the very best FD I can be'. There's no need to thank him!

#24

CONTEXT OF SESSION

Helping an Operations Director address behavioural issues with one of his senior managers ...

> COACH'S VOICE
>
> When trying to initiate a change think about the following three levels: is there enough suffering or reward for the individual to be motivated to change? Do they recognise and accept why they need to change – recognise the behaviour they are currently exhibiting and the consequences? Are they committed to a change in their behaviour?

#25

CONTEXT OF SESSION

Speaking with an ambitious senior leader (experiencing emotional trauma and anger) post having to let nine of his team go …

> ### COACH'S VOICE
>
> Consider how you could let go of your 'anger'. Think about the projection you are giving and the perception those senior stakeholders are building of you and your leadership style at this difficult time. Always consider the effect on your own career aspirations!

#26

CONTEXT OF SESSION

In helping a Head Of reflect on a traumatic financial year and a disconnected relationship with their outgoing boss …

> COACH'S VOICE
>
> What have you learnt about yourself this year? What has or will make you stronger? What changes do you wish to implement moving forward?

#27

CONTEXT OF SESSION

In assisting a Head Of (charity sector) begin to create a strategy for fundraising ...

> COACH'S VOICE
>
> Think business first! What type of events maximise your return on time and investment? This knowledge gives you the opportunity to communicate and clarify your focus and priorities to key supporters and volunteers, rather than be pulled into ad-hoc and numerous lower value events!

VOICE

APRIL

30

#28

CONTEXT OF SESSION

In helping a senior manager wanting to build his profile and exposure ...

> COACH'S VOICE
>
> Firstly, it's about visibility with the right audience. Who is the 'right audience'? What opportunities do you have to be visual? Secondly, and when with the right audience, it's about making memorable contributions: often this involves courage – saying what you think and why!

#29

CONTEXT OF SESSION

Helping a senior leader assess the value of their contribution to the business ...

> COACH'S VOICE
>
> What matters most to the business? In line with this, what is the most impactful topic that you can influence or control right now?

#30

CONTEXT OF SESSION

In observing a Medical Director rehearse for an important team meeting, where he is facilitating a session to obtain feedback from his people on what works/what doesn't within their current working practices/behaviours ...

> COACH'S VOICE
>
> Believe in the process of obtaining the feedback. Look comfortable and confident in using the technique. Remind yourself why you are doing it. What does it enable? What will it improve? What's the reward? What suffering does it stop?!

#31

CONTEXT OF SESSION

In helping a senior leader develop a mechanism for controlling their frustration and subsequent display of anger ...

> COACH'S VOICE
>
> Consider how you can break the automatic connection between stimulus (event happening) and your reaction. How can you build in choice between the two? Enabling you to think about and consider your response. Consider Peter Hill's STOP model: STEP BACK, THINK about your reaction, ORGANISE your thoughts and PROCEED.

#32

CONTEXT OF SESSION

Giving counsel to a Sales Director becoming increasingly frustrated with one of their in-country distribution managers (on target/on budget), regarding their lack of proactiveness and work ethic ...

> COACH'S VOICE
>
> Think carefully about not leading with your own values and ethics regarding ways of working! People work in different ways to get the job done! One size doesn't fit all! Their defence is likely to be 'I'm on target/on budget'. Your objective is to instil motivation to change the way they currently work. Not always monetary incentive! Helping them see benefits to changing their approach is key - consider sharing best practice which in turn will be creating an expectation from you! Work to understand their current approach - avoid jumping in with accusation!

#33

CONTEXT OF SESSION

Coaching a Marketing Director conflicted between pursuing her proposals for a more global role and greater ownership within her existing company, versus a potential opportunity with her previous boss in a major blue chip (no formal approach as yet) ...

COACH'S VOICE

What's your instinct telling you? What excites you more right now? How would not getting your global role with your current company impact your decision? How could you manage your relationship with your previous boss in line with the timeline for your global proposals? What is your deadline for a decision on your internal proposals?

#34

CONTEXT OF SESSION

In helping a Head Of Marketing recover and forward focus following his unsuccessful internal application for the Marketing Director role ...

> *COACH'S VOICE*
>
> What feedback have you received from the appointing stakeholder? ('None, I haven't wanted to hear it'). What do you think you would be told? Is there any feedback that would frighten you? What if they could help you understand your 'blind spot' – giving you the opportunity to grow from this experience? I guess stay here bitter or stay here informed?!

#35

CONTEXT OF SESSION

In helping a Head Of Human Resources develop their strategic relationship and synergy with the CEO ...

> COACH'S VOICE
>
> Which of your peers has the most formed strategic relationship and synergy with the CEO? What is it they are doing? How can you carry your influence and gain the CEO's 'ear'?

MAY

3

#36

CONTEXT OF SESSION

In helping a Head Of Sales develop a robust and pragmatic 'induction' programme for a new starter in their account management team ...

> COACH'S VOICE
>
> Laying strong foundations for success is critical. Get your new starter to develop a fascination for their statistics. An acute knowledge of their call performance – number of calls made, duration of calls, objective achieved, results obtained etc. Understanding this data helps enable optimum performance.

#37

CONTEXT OF SESSION

In evaluating the success of a key priority ongoing project team (volunteer group working outside of business as usual) with the lead ...

> ### COACH'S VOICE
>
> Get your team together and discuss success and progress against the objectives over the last 12 months. Use the meeting to reset targets for the next 12 months. What are our 'drop dead' three priorities that we will judge ourselves on? Respect that the group is made up of 'volunteers' working outside their business as usual requirements – ask if they want to commit to the higher demands over the next 12 months and sign up their involvement. Use this to re-establish alignment and accountability.

#38

CONTEXT OF SESSION

In helping a Head Of Operations consider options for dealing with a talented but behaviourally non-compliant direct report ...

> COACH'S VOICE
>
> What is the consequence to their behaviour? What do you fear by having a consequence conversation? What could be the consequence to their actions? People change because of suffering or reward!

#39

CONTEXT OF SESSION

Listening to a CEO deliberating how to coach a 'disgruntled and insecure' direct report following a recent challenging event ...

> **COACH'S VOICE**
>
> Reception to change only really happens when an individual is stable and secure. If an individual is unstable and insecure it's probably not the right time to coach. You require the person to have psychological mindedness.

#40

CONTEXT OF SESSION

Discussing with a project manager his approach to fulfilling his career aspirations ...

> COACH'S VOICE
>
> How many of your skills as a project manager can be utilised to help you achieve your career ambitions? Consider seeing your career as a 'project' - applying an acute focus and execution to the elements that will achieve the end goal.

#41

CONTEXT OF SESSION

Discussing the career ambitions of a Learning and Development Professional, struggling to find a way to position her strengths at an interview ...

> COACH'S VOICE
>
> What are your top three strengths? What do they enable? Which of those three do you apply successfully the most? Would others say you hold the same strengths?

#42

CONTEXT OF SESSION

Assisting a Director in obtaining greater clarity and direction from their new 'hands-off' boss ...

> ### COACH'S VOICE
>
> Don't wait for direction, go first! Demonstrate your intellect, accountability and control. Consider setting the agenda for your next one-to-one. Think through and position your perception of your objectives and the priorities. Seek feedback and alignment from your boss and be willing to debate alternative views.

#43

CONTEXT OF SESSION

In helping a Commercial Director debate whether he should be coaching or mentoring a direct report ...

> COACH'S VOICE
>
> It's a question of where their knowledge base on a given area sits. If they have the knowledge on a given topic – look for opportunities to coach intelligent and innovative thinking from the individual. Never accept apathy and lazy thought from your direct reports, but if there isn't the knowledge base it may be appropriate to mentor at first. Pure coaching is at its most effective once a foundation of knowledge is laid.

#44

CONTEXT OF SESSION

In helping a Director Of Marketing 'sell' their career ambitions ...

> COACH'S VOICE
>
> Be more deliberate and certain with your career wants. If you don't know what you really want - nobody else will! In a sentence how would you position your career ambition to me?

#45

CONTEXT OF SESSION

Speaking with a Director Of Operations in receipt of consistent feedback from several new key stakeholders ...

> COACH'S VOICE
>
> **Feedback received:** 'They are a complex character, hard to approach and defensive at times'.
>
> Do you see what they see? Which part of the feedback would you like to change? How would you like it to be? Where do we start?

VOICE

JUNE

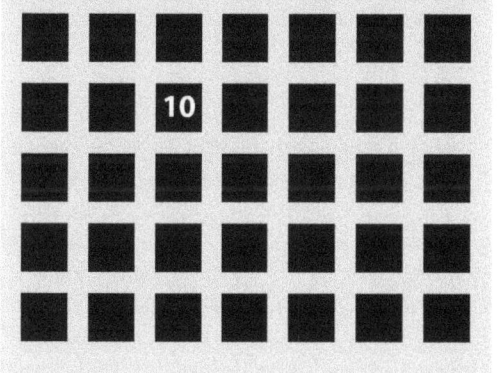

10

#46

CONTEXT OF SESSION

In coaching a senior leadership team on the receipt of potential redundancy news that could impact them as well as their people ...

> COACH'S VOICE
>
> You will interpret and reflect on what you've just been told differently. Allow yourself the time to internalise and adjust. Understand the risk of positioning to others if your mind is unstable and insecure. When it comes to positioning the time sensitive message to your managers later today – don't over elaborate in a time when you are still adjusting. Think about the essential content and delivery of your message but also your core initial objective. You should be empathetic, but others will look to you for your steadiness – what you say and how you look are equally important!

#47

CONTEXT OF SESSION

Aiding a Director as he addresses his new team and plans the sell of his vision and desired culture ...

> COACH'S VOICE
>
> What do you mean by culture? If you boil down the word culture - it's about behaviours! What people say and do! Be specific with your team in finding desired behaviours - rules of engagement if you like.

#48

CONTEXT OF SESSION

In helping a Head Of reflect on a negative perception from some of their senior colleagues as a result of explicit challenge they had initiated at a recent senior leadership team meeting ...

> COACH'S VOICE
>
> Consider in future the benefits of pre-framing your challenge! Tell them your position, your view of the situation with a positive frame. Then articulate the challenge that you see within. Don't cut corners without letting others see your positive processing.

#49

CONTEXT OF SESSION

In discussing with a senior leader their propensity to take on too much ...

> COACH'S VOICE
>
> Learn to say 'no' more. Let go of some things in order to 'grow', as a leader! Growth for yourself and for your team! What three things can you let go of right now?

#50

CONTEXT OF SESSION

Speaking with an ambitious senior manager seconded for six months into a high impact customer facing role ...

> COACH'S VOICE
>
> What does success look like in six months? Taking out weekends you have circa 130 days to achieve your success factors! Would it help if we look at 30-, 60- and 90-day milestones?

#51

CONTEXT OF SESSION

Listening to a Director just having resigned and on his three-month notice period prior to moving onto a senior role in another organisation (and worried about working out his term with passion and energy) ...

> COACH'S VOICE
>
> How important is taking good energy and success into your next role? Think about your legacy ... what you want to leave behind! How about you create a 'last' 90-day plan – breaking down actions across tangible goals?

#52

CONTEXT OF SESSION

In helping a Marketing Director prepare for a critical feedback meeting following a verbal disengagement with their line manager (meeting called by the LM) ...

> COACH'S VOICE
>
> What are your reflections on what happened to create the disengagement? What part did you play in it happening? Regarding the meeting, what do you want the outcome to be? How would you like him to position it? What if he doesn't? What's at risk if you lose control of your emotion? What's your best response on receipt of the feedback? The most productive use of the meeting is to focus forward – what do you want the relationship to look like? What needs to change?

JULY

17

#53

CONTEXT OF SESSION

Speaking with a Commercial Manager angered following some tough direct feedback received from their line manager regarding their style ...

> COACH'S VOICE
>
> Tell me what are you thinking/what are you feeling regarding the feedback? Regardless of how it was delivered, what part of the feedback is true? What aspect of the feedback do you choose to listen to? What parallel feedback have you received in the past that synergises with this feedback? What part would you like to change right now?

#54

CONTEXT OF SESSION

Discussing with a Vice President their need for reinforcement/praise from a line manager who doesn't readily share ...

> **COACH'S VOICE**
>
> It's unlikely that we can change your line manager! But you can control how you feel about it! It starts with your thinking! Maybe you can obtain reinforcement from other sources (past experiences, recent communications with your team and stakeholders)? Also consider whether you give off a vibe of needing reinforcement? You are a strong individual – perhaps others don't think you need it so don't give it? Finally, you say you are generally suspicious of compliments in all aspects of your life ... many compliments will be genuine?! Make sure you receive and respond well!

#55

CONTEXT OF SESSION

In listening to a senior leader become increasingly frustrated at a perceived lack of growth opportunities within their organisation ...

> COACH'S VOICE
>
> Have you done 'your best' to state your ambition with key stakeholders in your business? In terms of stating your ambition, what's been 'your best'? What feedback have you received back? Having heard the feedback, what else can you do? What options do you have?

#56

CONTEXT OF SESSION

Discussing with a Head Of their individual profile and brand ...

> COACH'S VOICE
>
> If I didn't know you, what would I learn about you from your on-line profile? Let's take a look! Looking at their LinkedIn profile – what descriptive words and phrases jump out? Is that the profile/brand you are wanting? What do you want to change? In this digital age, consider the benefits of demonstrating 'thought leadership' in your organisation/industry ... How could this benefit your profile/brand?

#57

CONTEXT OF SESSION

Speaking with a senior leader concerned about their natural logical, factual, pragmatic and direct contributions in senior meetings and how they are received by others ...

> ### COACH'S VOICE
>
> Your strength is in your logical approach and risk assessment to given scenarios and challenges. But be careful not to overplay your strength! People need different things! Get used to reading the room and assessing readiness for your strength. Consider showing how you synergise with the positive frame of others at times, prior to challenging actions. Pre-framing your challenge shows consideration, appreciation and tact!

#58

CONTEXT OF SESSION

Working with a Human Resources Director concerned about a series of identified development areas of a peer, not registering with the CEO after a number of failed verbal attempts ...

> COACH'S VOICE
>
> What benefits are there to writing down the perceived development areas and sharing with the CEO? Benefits to you – clarity of thought, perhaps separating any noise that sits outside of core development priorities? Benefits to the CEO – a definitive list for them to digest and then choose how and if they want to deliver?

#59

CONTEXT OF SESSION

Talking with a Managing Director working hard to create a positive frame with Board stakeholders in a difficult landscape …

> COACH'S VOICE
>
> Be realistically positive – it's never all great! Show that you are aware of deficiencies but on top of the plan! Small cracks in the veneer are ok! No cracks in the veneer and senior stakeholders may become suspicious and in an extreme case … question your credibility!

#60

CONTEXT OF SESSION

In offering advice to a people centred Commercial Director, starting to strategically plan his regions and growth opportunity for the next quarter ...

> COACH'S VOICE
>
> Work off a blank canvas. Assess the growth opportunity within each region. Project income and turnover potential, but also assess the risks in-country: speed of product to market and in-country regulation for example. Remove your people from your thinking initially - the opportunity should drive the need first. Your people can then be mapped into the picture. This will help ensure your thinking is balanced with both logic and emotion!

VOICE

AUGUST

1

#61

CONTEXT OF SESSION

Speaking with a Marketing Director – thinking through his next career move ...

> COACH'S VOICE
>
> Many people I know will create a framework for their next career move – a blueprint if you like! You could use the framework as a structure to assess other career opportunities against, rather than just be courted by offers and make yourself fit!
>
> Just to share some feedback with you, this is the first time we have met – in 45 minutes and on four separate occasions, you have referred to your most enjoyable and successful time being a Director Of Sales! Should you be listening to this voice?

#62

CONTEXT OF SESSION

In helping a senior manager understand the impact of their pragmatic and direct risk assessment of other people's ideas within a senior leadership team meeting ...

> COACH'S VOICE
>
> Post framing your perceptions of the positive benefits of an idea after positioning your risk assessment in a direct way is likely to get a mixed response! Some colleagues will remember the risk you have positioned only - not hearing the balance you have applied! What value reversing your current approach? Positioning in a positive frame to get others on-board first before delivering the balanced 'but'. If you get others receptive to wanting to hear the 'but' - you may find it easier to influence? Not being unfairly seen as the 'negative guy'!

#63

CONTEXT OF SESSION

Scenario planning with a Head Of Service Management, regarding influencing his CEO to 'sign-off' his new operating model and structure ...

> COACH'S VOICE
>
> Sell me your case for change!
>
> To create a sense of urgency, focus on the risks to the business of inaction. Consider the rule of three – what three short and succinct statements motivate the CEO to buy into your proposed change? Keep statements factual and tie in effective data.

#64

CONTEXT OF SESSION

In helping a senior leader reflect and learn following their extreme emotional reaction in the face of a severe challenge a few days earlier ...

> COACH'S VOICE
>
> Tell me what the last few days, post incident, have been like for you ...
>
> What's the impact on you been? What about the impact on others? Where are you now? What are you feeling? What are you thinking?
>
> You have actually realigned and stabilised yourself. Is it about finding a coping mechanism that gets you there quicker? What part of your recovery approach can we implement quicker?

#65

CONTEXT OF SESSION

Challenging a senior manager to accept feedback from their team regarding their style and approach ...

> COACH'S VOICE
>
> Regarding your interactions with your team, describe you at your very best ...
>
> Tell me about your behaviours, style and mannerisms at your very best ...
>
> What impacts you from being the very best version of yourself?
>
> How often are you at your very best?
>
> What would you like your team to say about your style and approach going forward?
>
> What would you like to do more of/do less of that would positively impact your team?

#66

CONTEXT OF SESSION

Challenging a senior leadership team to finesse a very important stakeholder facing document essentially justifying their results and approach ...

> COACH'S VOICE
>
> Please allow me to share some feedback? Best of intentions as always! What I've heard is a lot of frustration, which has led to a very gutsy and robust response on paper. I can also see that some of you are uncomfortable with this approach ... a little anxious? What is the objective of the document? Is it worth revisiting the 'tone' of your response? Would a more balanced tone be received better? What are you prepared to finesse without losing the points you want to make?

#67

CONTEXT OF SESSION

Speaking with a robust and uncompromising International Markets Director experiencing a turbulent initial relationship with a new peer ...

> COACH'S VOICE
>
> When two senior people bring their own strong authentic presence to a new relationship, there is a probability that synergies and acceptance will take time to build. With challenge being at the heart of your presence ... it's important to take time to build and work the relationship first to enable your peer to see your intent and receive the challenge. There are no shortcuts!

#68

CONTEXT OF SESSION

Working with a Chief Operating Officer 'tempted' to apply for the soon to be vacant CEO role in an SME ...

> COACH'S VOICE
>
> What can you bring to the role? What will others miss about the outgoing CEO? What gaps do you see in yourself in readiness for performing in the role? How do you think your appointment would be received by others? What's your plan?

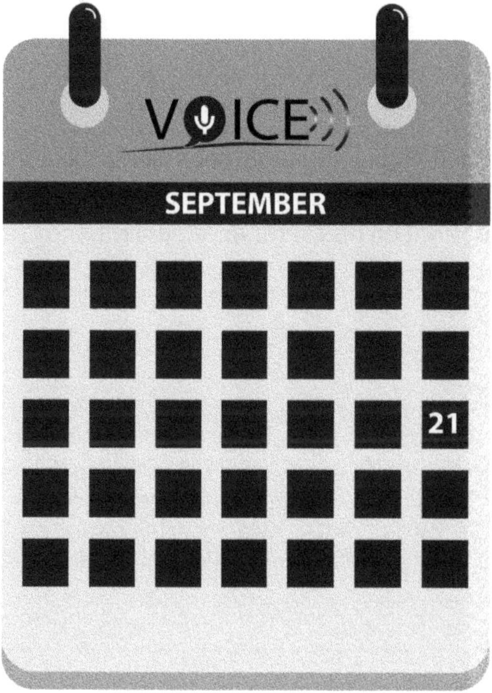
VOICE
SEPTEMBER
21

#69

CONTEXT OF SESSION

Challenging an ambitious senior leader (recognised as high potential by his organisation) on his career development ...

> COACH'S VOICE
>
> There is a 'price of entry' that determines your right to talk up your career ambitions with your superiors. Challenge yourself on the following three elements: are you delivering results that achieve your objectives? Are you exceeding the expectations of you by bringing added value? Are you demonstrating knowledge and depth outside of your technical specialism? From there you can develop your plan and engage.

#70

CONTEXT OF SESSION

In conversation with two business owners (partners) following two unsuccessful appointments to a 'generalist' senior management position ...

> COACH'S VOICE
>
> What has been the challenge? (the individuals were each good at some aspects, but poor at other key dependencies).
>
> In a sentence what is it you need from this position? Be specific.
>
> What three critical business elements must they excel at? Have you recruited in line with these three areas?

#71

CONTEXT OF SESSION

Helping an executive graduate reflect on his strengths and key skills – two years into his three year graduate scheme ...

> COACH'S VOICE
>
> What have you learnt about your strengths?
>
> What's not for you and why?
>
> How does this shape your future role?

#72

CONTEXT OF SESSION

Working with an executive graduate – preparing for his first experience of a networking event …

> COACH'S VOICE
>
> What are your expectations of the event?
>
> What are you excited about? What concerns you? What's important for the company? What does your introduction/greeting look, sound and feel like?

#73

CONTEXT OF SESSION

Speaking with an ambitious leader regarding their 'explicit' defence of a direct report in the face of some strong challenge from seniors about their sales performance ...

> COACH'S VOICE
>
> Your loyalty to your team member is commendable. Which aspects of the challenge from your seniors are true about your direct report? What are you aiming to achieve in your defence of them? The light always shines on you as the leader! Positioning is key – is there a way to acknowledge the challenges your direct report is facing, whilst at the same time promoting some of the individuals' strengths, and actions you are working through? This balance will show your control of the situation and if needed, help smooth the perception of your leadership.

#74

CONTEXT OF SESSION

Working with a member of a talent pool disappointed with the lack of opportunity for career growth following membership to the pool ...

> **COACH'S VOICE**
>
> Tell me what kind of control you are taking with your own career development plans?
>
> Being a member of a talent pool is an identification of your talent/potential. It's not a guarantee of career advancement. You are in a small pond but a very competitive one! Those that are taking proactive control and ownership will thrive and court opportunities. What could you do more of?

#75

CONTEXT OF SESSION

Speaking with a Head Of following challenge from their line manager regarding the value of two business development managers ...

> COACH'S VOICE
>
> So, the two individuals are on target/on budget yet the challenge has still come. What's the reason for the challenge – where is it driven from? Is it down to a perceived lack of ambition with their targets, or the need to reduce costs and lessen the expense of the roles? It's important that you get clarity so you can manage the situation/your line managers expectations.

VOICE

OCTOBER

18

#76

CONTEXT OF SESSION

Listening to a Head Of Distribution anxious about the arrival of a senior consultant – briefed by the CEO to help structure and future proof the distribution and sales section ...

> COACH'S VOICE
>
> View this as a partnership. Reach clarity early on objectives, approaches, rules of engagement, permissions etc. Share your concerns. Alignment at an early stage avoids blurred lines. Show your team that you are 'together'.

#77

CONTEXT OF SESSION

Helping a senior manager seek clarity on whether to exit their existing role in favour of a comparative role within another organisation ...

> COACH'S VOICE
>
> Where has your thinking taken you? What's your gut feel? What's proving difficult in your decision? What would make it easier? If your friend was in the same situation with the same dilemma, what counsel would you give them?

#78

CONTEXT OF SESSION

Speaking with a Director serving his notice prior to joining a new global brand ...

> COACH'S VOICE
>
> What are your key immediate priorities in your new role? Would it benefit mapping these priorities across your first 30-, 60- and 90-days?
>
> What would you like to 'tweak' about you in preparation for this new leadership position? What would you like to be even better at?

#79

CONTEXT OF SESSION

Coaching a Regional Director in receipt of a mandate from their C-suite executives to reduce headcount and let a significant earning and close colleague go ...

> COACH'S VOICE
>
> Firstly, it's important to understand the decision-making rationale of the C-suite. You'll need backbone to deliver the message but don't forget to listen to your heart - you have history so be empathetic. Empathy means understanding the impact the news will have on the individual, but not blaming others for the decision. Manage your expectations with regards to the individuals' immediate reaction to the news. It's difficult to forecast how somebody will react, so see delivery of the news as a first step only - it may be highly appropriate to deliver the news and then reconvene a day later. Show your heart through the process but do be consistent with your message.

#80

CONTEXT OF SESSION

Listening to a CEO wanting to push themselves and their senior leadership team to 'world class' performance level next year ...

> COACH'S VOICE
>
> Describe what 'world class' looks like in your mind. Does your team share your vision? Where do you think you are right now in relation to your vision? What does the gap look like? What priorities will help close the gap? Where do you see obstacles and how do you navigate through them?

#81

CONTEXT OF SESSION

Speaking with a Sales Director with an appetite to 'control' those around them, and in receipt of feedback that describes them as a 'control freak' ...

> COACH'S VOICE
>
> Tell me how the feedback has landed with you. Do you recognise the feedback – what parts of the feedback do you see in yourself? Is that the perception you want to create? What perception do you want others to have of you? Why is that important, what does it enable?
>
> Wanting to add value to individuals is hugely commendable and there is certainly a time when it is needed. But nobody needs and wants it all the time! It is possible to add too much value!

#82

CONTEXT OF SESSION

Helping a Chief Operating Officer reflect on an award-winning year to date and prepare their senior team for a 'gigantic' even bigger push next year ...

COACH'S VOICE

Whilst it's important to acknowledge the blood, sweat and tears that have led to your positive results, it's critical to create a sense that the effort and commitment can be matched again. It becomes our norm - it wasn't an unsustainable one-off. We go again! It's our standard now. Great sporting teams possess the same quality - we win more! Some of the key questions to ask are - what have we learnt from this year? Despite our success what challenges did we face that were tough and might be even tougher next year? What new challenges will we face? What can we tweak in our strategy, approach and ourselves that keeps us winning?

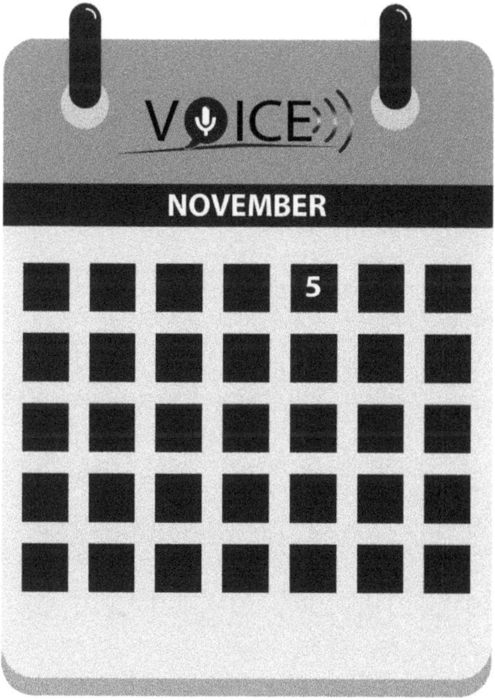
VOICE
NOVEMBER
5

#83

CONTEXT OF SESSION

Challenging a Regional Business Director to consider engaging with social media to aid his career ambitions ...

> COACH'S VOICE
>
> What is your Brand? Some would suggest that your Brand is what people see when they search for you on-line! What perception would your on-line and social media presence suggest? Would you be seen as an expert in your field? A thought leader? Do you stand out? If not, one of your competitors for your next role will stand out! A strong social media strategy can eventually promote you passively! What could you do more of to aid your ambitions?

#84

CONTEXT OF SESSION

Speaking with a Human Resources Director readying an internal interim replacement for the outgoing Sales Director, but with concerns about the impact the appointment may have ...

> COACH'S VOICE
>
> What concerns do you have for the individual stepping up into the Sales Director role? What risks do you see for the company? What messages/feedback will help the individual transition smoothly into the role? You have the perfect 'window of opportunity' to offer candour to the individual - they will be motivated by the potential promotion and are likely to be receptive to you holding the mirror up!

#85

CONTEXT OF SESSION

Coaching a self-badged 'reflectionary' and 'introverted' Operations Director on not losing their voice at senior leadership meetings ...

> ### COACH'S VOICE
>
> Tell me about how you currently carry your voice in those meetings. What opportunities are being lost by you and the business as a result of your current approach? How can you develop your comfort with saying more and maybe quicker to bring your intellect into the conversation? It's finding a way to influence amongst dominant voices ... maybe you can make a statement – for example, 'I have some interesting analysis and thoughts to share at the right time' – creating a platform for your voice? Or develop a code with a close peer in the meetings to create a segway for your message?

#86

CONTEXT OF SESSION

Listening to a Marketing Director being swayed by their line managers destructive thoughts on other key stakeholders ...

> COACH'S VOICE
>
> Whilst it's important to gain the insights of your line manager, the quality of your own relationships with these key individuals is likely to determine results. For this you will be judged regardless of what others think! Be empathetic to your line managers thoughts, but collate your own and 'find a way to play' with each stakeholder.

#87

CONTEXT OF SESSION

Helping a new senior manager prepare to deliver developmental behavioural feedback to a direct report and ex-peer ...

> COACH'S VOICE
>
> How would you describe your relationship with your ex-peer? Is it possible to be too close, too friendly with a direct report? You know you're too close when you simply can't find a way to deliver critical feedback! Finding a 'connected distance' is crucial in being able to manage them effectively. Maybe the relationship needs to be different now? How can you manage your initial discomfort with this?

#88

CONTEXT OF SESSION

Listening to a senior manager analysing his self-acclaimed 'disappointing' performance in a recent senior leadership team meeting ...

> COACH'S VOICE
>
> What were you disappointed with? Specifically, what was the trigger for your response? At that moment what were you feeling? What thinking led to that feeling? What were the consequences of your behaviour in the meeting? Your thoughts generate your feelings which in turn dictate behaviour ... the key in future is to control your thinking!

#89

CONTEXT OF SESSION

In helping a senior leader make the first steps towards applying for an internal promotion ...

> COACH'S VOICE
>
> It starts with stating your ambition! Making it clear why you want the role and what you can bring. In preparation for that, why do you want the role? What can you bring to it? As you know of a strong competitor for the role - what are their qualities? Without being disrespectful to any other applicant, in beating any competitors to the role - what's your 'weapon'? Your major selling point!

#90

CONTEXT OF SESSION

In listening to a Finance Director becoming increasingly frustrated by the lack of 'critical management information' being provided by their peers ...

> ### COACH'S VOICE
>
> What are you not getting from them that would make a significant difference to the role of you and your team? How does providing this to you aid their roles? Is the shortfall down to a lack of knowledge on their part or simply a choice they are making not to provide the information? If it's a knowledge gap – could a 'training' intervention from you help? If it's a 'will' issue – is there a consequence to the individual/team in not acting that could provide the motivation?!

#91

CONTEXT OF SESSION

Talking to a Distribution Director anxious about feedback given by the CEO to their line manager about their perceived lack of willingness/competence in leading a reduction in headcount ...

> COACH'S VOICE
>
> Is their truth in the feedback? To what degree? It's important that we understand the impact of this perception. It's human not to enjoy delivering difficult news! Preparing for the discussions is something we can talk about. In terms of managing the perception of the CEO, I think your line manager can help ... articulating back what you are doing in this area ... but alongside that it could be prudent to give regular updates directly to the CEO regarding where you are in the process, what you've done and your next steps?

#92

CONTEXT OF SESSION

Coaching a Sales Director wanting clarity on a rumoured strategy to sell off an operation they manage (one of many) in another country ...

> COACH'S VOICE
>
> What have you heard to date? How valid do you think the rumours are? How are you feeling about the rumours? What have you done to achieve clarity to date? It sounds like you need to focus on 'asking the right questions to the right people'. Firstly, who are the right people? What questions are relevant and the most important? It's important that you look ready to receive the news (whatever it is) when you address these 'right people'? You don't want to make them apprehensive - worried about your ability to receive the message ... you just need to know what it is?
>
> When can you do this?

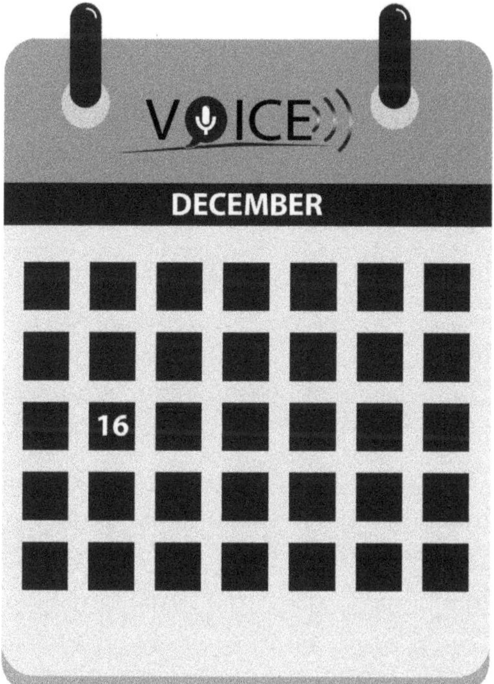

DECEMBER

16

#93

CONTEXT OF SESSION

Offering feedback to a senior leadership team following an observed meeting ...

> COACH'S VOICE (continued over)
>
> What went well today? What could have made the meeting even better? I have some observations that fall into the category of, 'even better if ...', would you like to hear them? If you think about the content and discussions of the meeting as a diagrammatical heat map of two circles – an outer circle that enables conversation around issues, challenges that are difficult for us to control, and an inner circle which offers focus, certainty, planning and action – where did you spend most of your time?

> **COACH'S VOICE**
>
> Spending time in the inner circle offers you more. We need awareness of the outer circle and doubtless some discussion, but being more deliberate and aware - moving to the inner circle quicker would have enabled more productive outcomes. Fair?

#94

CONTEXT OF SESSION

Speaking with a CEO, having difficulty pondering an internal appointment and selecting from two senior applicants ...

> COACH'S VOICE
>
> The selection process is vital - it should be fair and consistent for both. Fact. Both candidates need to feel that they have to perform on that stage.
>
> It is however natural to have an opinion on both candidates now - you work with both of them very closely.
>
> It's important to weigh up all the evidence with regard to their suitability for the candidacy, without getting too swayed by individual feedback from others about their style and substance. You can listen but much of that feedback can be subjective and with hidden agendas! Look for your intelligent intuition!

#95

CONTEXT OF SESSION

Working with a Director, 'stunned', 'apprehensive' and 'excited' by an invite to apply for the candidacy of CEO ...

> COACH'S VOICE
>
> What excites you about the opportunity? What do you see yourself bringing to the organisation? What's driving the apprehension? Why not you for CEO? How would you feel if you didn't apply and the opportunity passed you by? Would you suffer regret? If not now, when would you be ready to be a CEO?

#96

CONTEXT OF SESSION

Speaking with a newly appointed CEO following his successful application over a peer ...

> COACH'S VOICE
>
> What's your ex-peer thinking and feeling? What do you want them to say about your appointment? What messages will help you 'on-board' them? What outgoing message across the business will enable your ex-peer to move forward?

#97

CONTEXT OF SESSION

Listening to a Director express his concerns about two predicted internal applications from his team to a newly created post ...

> COACH'S VOICE
>
> Talk me through your major concerns. On hearing of their interest and intention to apply – what immediate feedback did you offer them? It's clear you see a gap in their capability and skill to perform in the new role ... expectation setting about their readiness for such a role and feedback regarding the 'gap' you see is critical in terms of their career development – whether this role or for the future. Honesty is key, not managing expectations and not offering feedback at the start carries a high risk if an internal candidate applies and is unsuccessful at whatever stage in the process. Hearing developmental feedback for the first time on rejecting their application is likely to be met with high emotion and disappointment!

#98

CONTEXT OF SESSION

Group coaching with a senior marketing team, and offering feedback following a complex and challenging activity that they failed to complete …

> COACH'S VOICE
>
> What was difficult and challenging about the task? Specifically, what caused you to fail? What would you do differently? Please let me share my thoughts …
>
> Acute planning at the start of the task was essential. In a task like that the probability of failure without deliberate and deep planning was high. You needed to identify potential challenges at the outset and scenario plan them – working through 'what would we do if … ?' type questions. Identifying challenges along the way having chosen a solution impacted time, energy and motivation. Apply your critical thinking earlier!

#99

CONTEXT OF SESSION

Challenging a rising-star with aggressive career ambition, to consider the impact of building his brand via social media engagement ...

> COACH'S VOICE (continued over)
>
> What is your brand? Your brand is what people find out about you when they 'Google'! Social media activity helps create a strong on-line footprint. People are now using social media to search for quality candidates and fill key positions. What opportunities are you missing by not even having a social media presence?

COACH'S VOICE

Professional business networks (like LinkedIn) allow you to promote your brand by effectively creating an on-line CV. Once your profile is loaded and you have gained professional connections, you can then engage via liking and sharing the posts of others, and creating your own. What would you want to 'post' about? What topics would enhance your brand? Perhaps you have the opportunity to be seen as a thought leader? What value could that bring to your career?

#100

CONTEXT OF SESSION

Readying a senior manager for the assessment process of a Head Of role ...

> COACH'S VOICE
>
> Let's anticipate the doubts/concerns of the assessment panel! As the role is to lead circa 200 people and you lead 40 at the moment, how would you compete against a more experienced people leader? How do you assess the 'gap'? What special qualities do you bring that negate any concern about your experience? What's your competitive edge?

COACH'S FINAL VOICE

A large percentage of a coach's work is preparing others to face their big events. Helping them not only plan, but also rehearse the execution of it. Challenging them to think with agility around a number of potential outcomes helps breed confidence for when they are about to take action.

You can coach pressure. And it's important that you do. You can help build an individuals' resilience by scenario planning through difficult situations – making the event seem real before it is live!

Your perspective can enhance their perspective. Challenging assumptions and complacency, and when appropriate offering a different lens to see things through can improve the quality of someone's thinking.

Nurture great 'teach ability' in those that you work with. Help them become students of their specialism – developing a thirst for more knowledge and skill. Foster a relationship where their continued development is bought into the sessions. It really helps!

Dean

Lightning Source UK Ltd.
Milton Keynes UK
UKHW010933240620
365466UK00001B/226